# THE REALMS AWAKEN

ALSO BY DELILAH SULLIVAN

*The Teachings of Mr P.*

*A Metaphysical Conversation with Rudyard Kipling:*
*On Writing, the Afterlife and the Spirited Human*

**BOOK ONE**
*Metaphysical Observations*

# THE REALMS AWAKEN

DELILAH SULLIVAN

PUBLISHED WORD
**PW.**

Published by: Published Word Ltd
27 Old Gloucester Street, London, WC1N 3XX

Text copyright © Delilah Sullivan 2025

This edition copyright © Published Word Ltd 2025

The moral rights of the author have been asserted, in accordance with the Copyright, Designs and Patents Act 1988.

All rights reserved. No part of this book may be reprinted or reproduced in whole or in part, stored in a retrieval system, or transmitted in any form or by any means, electronic, mechanical, photocopying, recording or other, now known or hereafter invented, without prior permission in writing from the publisher.

The information shared in this book should not be treated as fact or as substitute for medical advice. Neither the author, nor the publisher, prescribe the use of any ideas, techniques or suggestions in this book as a form of treatment for physical, mental or medical problems. Always consult a medical professional in matters relating to health. In the event you use any of the information in this book for yourself, neither the author nor the publisher can be held responsible for any loss, claim or damage as a result of suggestions made.

A catalogue record for this book is available from the British Library.

ISBN: 978-0-9955787-4-6
eBook ISBN: 978-0-9955787-5-3

Cover design and typesetting by Therese Vandling at @studiovandling

www.delilahsullivan.com

For my parents,
Jim and Carol,
with love and gratitude

The bravest act you will ever do is to follow
your Soul's calling. Guaranteed, it will torment you
at times. It will ravish your senses in moments of quiet
reflection and call you towards the great unknown.
And all this, within the faintest whisper, so soft ... you
may almost dismiss it as pure fancy.

**AG**

The passages in this book contain metaphysical observations and reflections from me, supported by quotations from my spiritual guides and metaphysical beings, often recognised as angels. Their presence is acknowledged in the 'With Gratitude' page towards the end of this book, and by their initials alongside each quote. Their wish, in contributing to this work, is to inspire the senses of the reader and awaken what is ready to emerge. I invite you to hold the words and energies lightly, at a distance and within you, as your own observations become true for you.

Love, Delilah

# 1

You are a ritual of the Realms – of the Realms you inherited and the ones you create. And of the Realms we share together. A living, moving fractal of the Divine.

# 2

There's a magic in the universe which feeds our soul and awakens our spirit. And it belongs to the Realms. You may have glimpsed it, interacted with it, or even communed with it – allowing it to move through you, as a way of living and breathing, of loving and creating. Perhaps you quietly dismissed it, with other things to do. Not quite ready for the illumination; not yet.

Our embodied presence contains this magic. We call it awakening, but really there's no other way to be; not if we truly wish to live the fullest experience of this reality. Our encounter with the awakening of our inner spirit – of an unexplainable expansion and simultaneous settling – usually happens without our noticing, initially that is, and often during times of crisis. It may be subtle and deliciously inviting, nudging you into new ways. Or it may tear your physical world apart, to reveal sudden or distressing change; the confusion, a temporary respite and a chance to breathe. Maybe, if you are fortunate, you never left the Realm of mystery. Or perhaps, you have yet to discover it. That's the exquisite beauty of it: the magical call within. Because, by the nature of our beating hearts, we are all disciples of the mystery.

# 3

The Realms carry information, revealed within sparks of understanding. Little whispers, spatial nudges, divine inspiration formed into ideas – simplicity and complexity to the untrained eye. But once we enter the Realms, new worlds emerge as we discover what, on some level, we deem to be becoming true. It is in the moments of chaos we gain perspective – and in the quietness we enter the wisdom. For the knowledge is never separate from our experience of it.

The difference when observing from *within* the energies of the Realms is that we also see the bigger picture. And that is when the healing happens, and when the healing informs.

# 4

My awakening happened in 2011 during a diagnosis of cancer. Suddenly a force field of Realms awakened and moved through me, blowing my world apart. Time was instantaneously collapsing, sucked through me into a disappearing vortex. With my past no longer a viable reference and my future a rapidly disappearing reality, I was inadvertently dropping into the present moment. I cannot tell you how long this took, maybe minutes, maybe hours, maybe days – until a loud echo told me I had arrived. *'Now the real work can begin.'*

My soul had spoken.

For the first time in my life, I was listening.

The channel was open.

# 5

*The discomfort is proof you are ready.*

MR P.

A crisis is not a requirement for awakening – because Love will take you there. In Love's unique way. Most likely you are already on the path ... have noticed the tell-tale signs: the silent questioning; the discomfort with what has worked its way into your life without your heart's permission; the draw and awe of beauty, supported by the whispers – the sense of *feeling* in a new way. You may also, perhaps, sense anger – suppressed and directionless – and noticeable separation from what was once strived for. Or you may feel nothing: numb, for safety.

And *this* can also be a crisis.

Because a new world is waiting for you.

# 6

The Realms make themselves known slowly at first, and then with insistence. Because we can be stubborn, can't we? Or petrified. Of what we might have to let go of. What we have worked so hard for: the inherent sacrifice of our life to date.

Our younger self may have heard the call – an otherworldly invitation behind momentary words – or stood awestruck in wonder, then turned away. Months, years can pass – mini timelines of our living in the presence of doorways to a greater dimensionality of ourself. The known stranger in our lives, walking beside us – beckoning, consoling our resistance, holding the threads.

A presence within its disappearance.

## 7

> ME: ... *how long will that take?*
> GUIDE: *As long as is needed ... and it will come too soon.*

It was cancer which called me into my body, but it was my newly discovered heart which took me to meet it. A necessary transformation had begun; however, it was my heart's permission which enabled the unequivocal acceptance. Heart, soul, my shattered ego – an ego which was no longer able to protect me – all found their way into my body.

When we go within, we cross a threshold – while simultaneously expanding through other restrictions in our life. One cannot happen without the other: you are multidimensional. Take care with this process; go slowly and collect the invisible pieces of yourself first. Hold them lightly, but preciously, and keep space for the pieces you will find on the other side.

## 8

*To discover your true self, you must
accept your true self.*

MR P.

We cannot discover the Realms through the eyes of another. And we can only see what we permit ourselves to see – to the degree of our acceptance. But a glimpse can become a stream. A glimpse can change your life. Because what the Realms show you cannot be unseen.

# 9

*What is <u>useful</u> is what we explore – only what is useful. This is the path within you.*

MR P.

When exploring the Realms, choose only to experience what is useful. Useful according to your heart and path, not your head or fears. Not your ego-mind or what others find useful to them, but what calls to be revealed or settled within you. Identifying the increasingly compelling is a quality of awakening. Let the eagerness of promise, of silent encouragement, nudge you forward. And as for what you collect: let it remain 'unsolved' in your awareness, an oscillating piece of a larger tapestry within you.

# 10

*Raise your intention to meet your reflection in its highest esteem, not its lowest.*

MR P.

Beneath the layers lies our truth. Alive, moving; influencing our state of being. Ready to emerge, though we may not be.

So we cultivate fluidity. By noticing our intention and orientating ourselves towards bliss and ease – *towards* the highest states – while releasing any resistance to this orientation. And allowing all other emotions to be. It is an agility and willingness to move within and between *all* emotional states, to allow them to merge and flow – without underestimating this act of non-attachment. Because to rest in bliss can be as challenging as it is enticing to remain within the comfort of disharmony.

## 11

*The magic is there, but you have to
go through the heart.*

DG

To access the magic we must first emerge from the energy of survival – and from the comfort of disharmony. From the patterns and thought-forms which once kept us safe. What is true for you *in this moment*? Are you seeing the world as fundamentally benevolent, or as dangerous? Are the people you live amongst inherently good, or not? Not what you *should* feel, or logic – or what your loved ones feel – but what is actually true in your heart.

Beneath it all – the trauma, the life experiences, the unspoken loyalties and energetic and familial systems – lies the axis of our orientation.

What we find may surprise us.

## 12

*The Realms are benevolent ... if you
will allow them to be so.*

MR P.

My awakening revealed many contrasting perspectives, but none more surprising than the newly effervescent feeling of joy. Although I had a sudden and aggressive cancer, for the first time in my life I felt out of danger.

I had moved from survival to inspiration.

And none of it made sense.

What did make sense, however, was that I had never felt so alive, so well or so beautiful.

## 13

*Safety requires a new consciousness of Spirit.*
*It is within you.*

MR P.

To heal, we must first accept our reality. We can't heal from where we don't want to be. When we try to avoid – or subtly tell ourself things are not as they are – we leak power into an energetic mass of our own making, holding 'life' in a compromised way. Accepting reality, as it is, is how we let go. No noise, no stories. A spiritual kneeling at the altar of Life, to a power much larger than ourselves.

This surrender to the truth within us is not done to 'change ourselves' or our circumstances – it cannot come with *any* conditions – but as an act of ultimate presence: of witnessing ourself in pure form, as we are, in all-that-is.

Now we are in alignment.

Now we can direct the energy from *the safe ground*.

## 14

*Staying close to the ground – to <u>her</u> ground – she
takes the moment to observe the world around her
and to where she is called.*

DG

To respect your mind, you must also respect your feet. This is what grounds you into the information and force fields – and earths your electricity. Keep this connection above all else. Always return to and start from yourself. Otherwise you are in energetic deficiency and delusion. Your mind is diverted; unavailable for the inspiring call.

## 15

*We change the energy fields with our awareness.*

DG

When we open our minds, we come alive. This is what awareness is. And yet it's more. It is a moment of dropping into ourselves, which we carry to the next – and every – moment. Awareness builds ... and releases: as the new comes into awareness itself. It is presence, compassion and deliberate intent. And it is very powerful.

It is also empty, with a quality of rigour which keeps it fresh and enticing. Awareness has no expectation, but holds wonder ... of all space and all potentiality. It is beyond time, softly encompassing the known.

Awareness comes to us when we are ready to receive. It is as unconditional in its invitation as we must be to receive it. You know when you're in it because you are observing and moving from a different perspective. Or even no perspective at all.

## 16

*The non-physical is counterbalance
to the physical.*

MR P.

With the cultivation of awareness, we attend to the needs of what cannot be seen. Words, sounds, rhythms of indescribable symmetry and song guide us – forward and into stillness. A song, beginning. And in letting the unspoken be the voice, giving rise to new information, we facilitate the opening of our channel with the Realms. Observed by our awareness, we witness a conversation developing. A conversation of such purity, we *know* the angels are watching.

17

*The forces conspire to support you.*

RK

The experiences which have meaning tend to simultaneously require more, *and* less, from us. *More* from the unseen worlds and *less* from ourself. We might experience this as letting go; however, there are no vacuums in the reality of Realms. When we drop our resistance and defences, and trust in our ability to discern, the Realms come to our assistance.

Because we have let them in.

## 18

*Tranquillity is dynamic.*

MR P.

There is a stillness in Nature which offers a doorway. A portal to resplendent layers of technicolour vibrancy. It is an invitational doorway, permitted through the trinity of your clean and unhindered presence, Nature's participatory consent and the instigation of the Realms. One must ask, without asking; and leave without leaving. It is an understanding inherent to the nature of reality.

In the absence of other options, make Nature your place of worship. You will not be alone.

19

*Freedom is the sound of the universe.*

DG

Connecting with the Realms is as listening to music. It comes to you, the song approaching.

Sometimes we catch distant words; floating by, carried across waves of sound. And sometimes we listen deeper. Called inward, into the layers. Into the beat, the energy behind the lyrics, the meaning beneath – its sacredness joining chords within us. Somewhere, deep in the recess of our being. Of a moment – a memory lived or a desire unlived; each equally powerful – and into something beyond.

## 20

*Become caretaker of your perception.*

**MR P.**

Pay attention to the whispers of heart, when the combined worlds pause and a gateway opens. These moments are for you, and you alone. Only you can answer the call … and slip into a new world. Only you.

When you do, the Realms will take care of you.

## 21

*The observation makes it real.*

**THE ELDERS**

There is a quality of Light which indicates an awakening Realm. You may sense it around you, within you – or in another. When you notice this lightness in others, pause, into the purity of the moment and the connectivity of the Realms.

For what you see in others is a reflection of what is within you.

## 22

*When one world transitions, another appears.*

DG

To perceive shifting worlds, we remove ourselves from 'time' and, instead, connect with the space. Words do not appear according to time, but from within space. Worlds, too. As we tend to our awareness, they begin to appear. Subtly at first – perhaps no sound, no sight, no feeling – but a co-creation is beginning. Because we have given permission.

When my world collapsed, it took all noise with it. In the silence, I found my voice – a voice I didn't know I was looking for, or even that it existed. I began writing ... words landing from the ether of an unknown yet familiar place. I was in a co-creative vortex of energies – and my heart was at the centre of it.

I was unravelling in order to discover. And it was exhilarating.

23

*Drop into softness.*

RK

For realities to emerge, we may need to adjust our senses or fine-tune our energy field. Collect and soften the corners of your life. Because there are no hard edges within the Realms.

## 24

*The heart is the most underused organ in the human body – even though it beats for you.*

AG

The Realms can be found in our heart – and our heart can be found in the crevices and expansiveness of our being. Larger than any thought, it is the gateway through which we experience the world. Our connection to the web of Love.

And, by the nature of its power, it can also be the most defended part of our psyche. Impenetrable by others – and often ourself: we live in danger of never experiencing its capacity, or even its blossoming. Trapped, beyond the present moment.

*Ever so slightly* out of reach.

# 25

The opening of my heart revealed a new terrain. One I had not walked or operated in before. Of desert wasteland coming to life. Layer upon layer, emerging into vision. Texture, feeling, new sounds and intonations. Colours and sensations – rising and flowing within me. And I was the central character. It was *my* reality, as I had never experienced it before. I felt alive with gratitude – and also torn. For my loved ones and the world I didn't want to leave. So my soul took me higher, and my need to write became essential. To make sense of what was happening, but also to understand this energy I was feeling. What I would come to understand as Love.

## 26

*What needs to stay, stays.*

**MR P.**

Turn away from yourself ... and you disconnect from your soul energy. It can be the subtlest of shifts, imperceptible to the human eye. But the inner sight sees every nuance, every movement of the senses. Especially what we try and hide from ourselves.

## 27

*You will not hear someone who is living
their truth ever talk of lack of time.*

MR P.

A reorientation occurs when we move out of clock time and position ourself within the multidimensionality of our soul. With clock time now at our disposal – and used to *create* flow – we are grounded in a larger world of possibility. Moment to moment, able to choose. No longer contracted by time, we breathe lighter. Even when the moments gather.

And, being human, we also fall out of alignment. Having enjoyed the expansive feelings of flow, a contraction will feel *even more* disconcerting and challenging to the senses. But we don't turn away or seek to escape from ourself. Because beneath every contraction lies wisdom wishing to emerge. Our job – the priority of our focus – is to guide ourself back into alignment. As lightly and swiftly as possible. By letting go. And then, in its own time, the wisdom will emerge.

The skill is not 'to stay in alignment'; the skill is in knowing how to return to ourself and our *evolving* alignment. The more adept we become at this, the wider we can explore; and ultimately, the more centred we become.

## 28

*Magic exists. If you allow it.*

RK

The magic happens at the edge of our comfort zone – not in the grand escapes of an action thriller. We want a wide vision, yes. But we must also, and deliberately, visit the near edges. These are the golden steps which unlock cosmic pathways and forces. It is not so much about 'what happens' at the edge, but going *to* the edge and meeting its energy there. When we step – and tentatively and cautiously is okay – to the threshold of nothing more than a sensation – of the sense of *something else* going on – the cosmic doors slide open, and we are met with the familiarity of our conscious and unconscious dreams. Now, the visioning becomes real.

The art is knowing how to dance at this threshold.

## 29

*Allow information to come to you.*

MR P.

The Realms are synchronicitous – so much so, we may not notice them. But settle into yourself a little more and you will begin to notice the adjusting qualities and nuances within them. What is wishing to come through, to make itself known? Can you simply breathe with it – as you are? And as it is. This is all that is needed for the connection to spark.

## 30

*Follow your dreams, for they are of the Realms.*

DG

Your subconscious is always guiding you ... the things you collect and place, which, almost mysteriously, find themselves in your orbit ... the title of a book staring at you from the shelf, almost pleading for you to pick it up ... the pictures, images, hidden meanings in the symbols of your life.

The question is not 'if' the symbols are there, more so ... *can you see them?* Can you look through the lens of the message to see the manifestation of it in your reality ... already there ... already conversing with the aspect of you not yet invited to you, by you?

# 31

*Trusting in the Realms enables the Realms to be.*

MR P.

The art of awakening is to develop a 'body of trust'. To listen, to curiously enquire, and lightly and lovingly hold ourself – *as we are*. As the conversations deepen *within* the body, our ability to explore expands: we begin to allow, *and feel*, our energies – and our experience of them. We trust because we accept the feedback into our body and energy field *as true*. We can forage for intentions, delve into new territories, learn to receive – because our body is learning to trust *us*. It is the most sacred of relationships because, as we develop a body of trust, the absence of fear creates the conditions for love.

## 32

Trust is an act of presence. Because it can only be experienced in the moment. So we take the smallest steps of conscious intentions and simple awareness, of presence for *this* moment. The answer for *this* question, as it arises, always with ourself at the centre. It's not about 'trusting another' or the past or the future, but taking our wisdom from within. From our source, just for this moment, with reality as it is.

When I had cancer, I *trusted it*. I became grateful for it. Something told me to, and I trusted this *something*. This something was part of me – stronger than me. Wiser than me. And not separate. I enjoyed the feeling trust gave me, the expansiveness which was possible when I tended to each moment and the choice within it; the mystery and possibility everything sat within. And when the fear gripped me, it told me, don't try to trust. Instead, let go – gather and organise yourself toward neutrality – back into the place of gratitude.

Because trust and gratitude go hand in hand.

## 33

*The oriented Soul has multiple options, but it
makes its choices to fulfil human intervention, too.
All possibilities; all outcomes.*

AG

It is not just our body we must learn to trust, but our soul, too. Trusting our soul is a prerequisite for a soul-led life. It wants the best for you. It came here to experience *this* life – to live and express itself through your physicality – to commune with your body and heart. Beautifully and imperfectly, as you are now. Not groundless, waiting; but as an embodied, co-creative force of *your* nature.

## 34

*In all, one finds one's way.*

AG

When we open to the Realms our resistance transmutes into a question. We move from *'I can't ...'* to *'please will you help me – show me how I can ...?'*

We move from −1 to +1. And in this reorientation, everything changes.

The forces flood in.

When the metaphysical is included, change feels good – even if it's hard or uncertain. Because our soul is included – doing what it came here to do.

## 35

*Let the forces accumulate in new ways.*

MR P.

When the Realms awaken, things start to move differently – because our energy field is shifting and changing in accordance with our higher self. As we look up, the forces sweep in to support us. They take the weight from us. The props, addictions and constrained behaviours of *our* force needed to 'hold it together' begin to melt away. Instead, we raise and widen our vision, to include the forces within all we do.

## 36

*It is mastery of energy in accordance
with one's Higher Self.*

MR P.

We cannot be present for reality if we are not present for ourself. So we call in all aspects of our spirit, to come and find their place in the sphere of our being. We retrieve, welcome and heal the pieces making their way to us – each fragment, an essential part of our magnetic core. Each piece, knowing when to slot into place, invisibly moving between Realms – within the symmetry and beauty of all things – into the essence of our being.

## 37

When the Realms awaken, our vibration begins to increase. Our perceptions become more sacred, liberated – and so, too, does our energy; with noticeable feelings of calmness, expansion and an inner freedom of movement. At its highest, we radiate a subtle luminosity: of Light – suspended and emanating – within our energy field. Our body enjoys this feeling, and in response, our essence radiates – with no effort required. People begin to notice – may smile as they pass – their gaze softening and widening, as they unconsciously recognise the presence of *something* they know to be true.

We are resonating at a different level. And this is attractive.

## 38

*It is the essence of you which*
*'manages your energy'.*

MR P.

Higher vibrations come with a wish to protect them; but we don't do this by hiding our energy or shutting down parts of ourself. Instead we protect our energy by allowing it to be its fullest, most divine force – as a gentle hum. Never in judgement or antagonism to other forces, but absolutely as it is: our essence, at its purest and fullest.

## 39

*Learning comes to us when we
have something to let go of.*

DG

Despite our best intentions, we can be a little hard on ourselves, can't we? As the Realms shift and move within us, our light reveals hidden shadows. After the momentary and extended highs, any denser energies will feel heavy – especially if they are entangled, or if the ego-mind jumps in. Patterns of control – which previously protected and enabled our safety – become out-dated; and we quickly, and sometimes painfully, discover we cannot direct or instruct the energies away.

Instead, we sit with them – and care for them gently.

By listening.

To them, and to our heart.

## 40

*The body will always benefit from
the lightest of touch.*

MR P.

When you feel gritty or experience static energy in the body, give yourself permission to let go. Let go and raise your intention to the *desired* feeling – not the one you don't enjoy. Whilst also caring for what needs to be cared for. Ask the forces to come and support you – to assist you in transmuting the energies; for what wishes to be healed – in service of the whole.

Healing is the domain of the angelic. Welcome and thank them in the little moments of higher vibration, knowing the denser energies are shifting in the background. You will know they are there, because you will sense it – a lightness, as your essence moves back into alignment. A softening and an exhale.

And then, the wisdom comes.

Because when energy shifts, reality shifts too.

## 41

*To know of the challenge, one is the Light. What is darkened is within – out of reach. Temporarily 'stilled'. It is this stillness which, given the conditions of awareness and a gentle sight, comes to be known as Love through the open heart. How this heart looks: battered; bruised; crushed deeply, perhaps – matters not when the beam is allowed to erupt. Stillness, stillness – and you will find a new force.*

AG

If you can accept, you have life. You don't have to like what is accepted. You don't even need to like yourself – or know what 'acceptance' is. We just ... let go of the struggle. Here, now ... as it is. Because when the struggle is contained – and maintained – we bleed energy internally.

But if we can accept – even when we don't know what it is or how to do it – we begin an awakening. The bleeding slows, then stops. The faint patter of an echo comes to greet you: of a heart unknown, yet familiar. And a stillness, which must be protected. Somehow, you know this.

In our ending, a new life is begun. That you may have died in this way many times before, adds to the reminder that your soul is knocking, gently, for your attention.

You are entering the world of the metaphysical.

## 42

*It's a powerful day, yes ... but no more than
any other. It's the energies which are powerful.
Don't credit the day with the energies.*

MR P.

When grounded in grace, we see the day *and* we see the energies: unique from each other. Each day becomes a living experience, a connection to the underlying gravity of presence; the energies as fascinating and powerful as they are malleable.

# 43

*'What does this experience wish to show me?'*
*This is the question which keeps us free.*

**DG**

The Realms show us true power. Not the kind which involves another, but the power within. Of truth, and ease, and discernment. We learn how, and when, to express this power – by discovering our inner dial. Because there are moments to turn the volume up, and there are many moments to turn it down.

So we can protect ourself and others.

And, most importantly, so we can ensure the flow.

## 44

*Be committed to the presence which sustains you.*

DG

Our world is bound by divine creativity. When we carry out our day's work in harmony with the Realms, we create families, homes, organisations and communities ... which time *adds* to. Outcomes of beauty and resonance, which *hum with energy*. When we plant a tree, sow a field, create a piece of art or music – or an aspect of ourself – with this intention, we add to the nature of reality, in flow with life. Time *imbues* it with content and richness.

We also know what it feels like to create *against* the flow of life: from an energy of fear or greed – or in service of forces of a different kind. We know what it feels like to create into the void of diminishing time.

It lacks energy and resonance.

45

*We alchemise reality through our presence.*

DG

We are vibrational communicators – between each other and between worlds. Transformers of higher frequencies down into matter. And denser energies up into Light. Each thought, or beautiful word uttered, a gateway of alchemy.

It is a power we are not accustomed to using – but one inherent within the nature of reality. Everything you see – *everything* created around you – happened in this way.

## 46

To observe the Realms is to transform Light into form. It comes with responsibility, for what we create attaches itself to the world around us. Even if only in thought – especially if only in thought. For our thoughts begin in invisible Realms, becoming visible to the world at large. In our eagerness to exercise our power, we must remember we operate in worlds capable of alchemy and destruction. The responsibility must not scare us, but awaken its true meaning within us.

# 47

*Do not carry a load that is not for you.*
*Do not carry a load which is not yours – or even*
*another's. There is nothing in vibrational unity which*
*requires a single approach. No thing, no thought, no*
*action. The vibrational unity takes this 'responsibility'*
*from your shoulders and sets you free to become who*
*you are. This is the way of the path. This is the*
*counterbalance to your brilliance.*

**THE ELDERS**


Your soul has an energy – is a beacon of Light, waiting patiently for you to shine with it. For you to embrace the Light, rather than the illusional responsibilities of the collective ego-mind. Help soothe and release the ego-mind, by not carrying unnecessary energetic weight.

Instead, connect with the Earth and seek wisdom from your path.

Your soul will find you there.

48

*You are the keeper of your Soul.*

DG

To be a conduit for the passing energy, we must first ground ourselves. Into the physicality of our planet and the reality of our essence. By becoming keeper of our wisdom: of a piece of wisdom so small and simple in its vastness, you probably overlooked it. Of a wisdom you may not be able to voice – and which may not be ready *to* be voiced – but, if you take a moment to pause, resonates through all dimensions of your being. A new centre of gravity: so you can stand within your own footsteps – the shadow and the light.

This is how the Realms reveal themselves – how the portal cuts through the noise.

## 49

### Cohabiting with the Divine

DG

We all have non-physical sources of guidance. Sometimes it's the weather, or a virtual voice through a phone. At other times, it's the thoughts in our head, or peer pressure. Our fears and our inspiration. Most of us are managing all of this, and more. Often without questioning the source or the energy of our guidance.

*And* we can cohabit with the angelic if we wish to. If we also give them space.

## 50

*Spirit is here to empower you,
not the other way round.*

MR P.

Upon meeting my spiritual guide, I became apprentice to his teachings. A contract was formed across the Realms. I was 'up-grading' energetically, while 'down-loading' information. And in the blink of an eye, I became 'a channeller'.

The first teaching was to become competent at moving within 'the field of Randomness' – to allow myself to be guided, with potentiality, while remaining in full awareness and grounded presence.

We call it flow.

And it happens when we let go.

## 51

*Go with the experience you wish to have.*

RK

When we let go, our life force reorientates itself. Because holding on pins us into a moment and a feeling – and our spirit becomes twisted, no longer facing forwards. But when we let go, however briefly, everything shifts around us. The energies flow back into alignment and our intentions – through a feeling of safety – begin to rise.

We are facing ahead, so now we can choose.

Because, whatever the action, we can only intend *forwards*.

## 52

*It is the energy behind the
intention which matters most.*

MR P.

When we fall in love with the energy behind our intention, everything changes. We cross a threshold in our heart – into the timeline of our soul. And from this perspective, we see our human lifetime – and the lifetimes of others – as the mystical wonder they are. We awaken to the living energy in all things. Because, when we fall in love with our life, part of us also falls in love with everyone and everything.

## 53

*The Realms are accessible to you
with instant effect and in your own time.*

DG

You do not need to sacrifice yourself for the Realms or tread on uncommon ground. Neither do you need to change anything about your life now, though you may wish to. Perhaps you do not believe the aspirations they suggest, and also you do not disbelieve them – as humans, we can struggle with what is 'ours' and what is not, can't we? The ego needs to know this ... but your soul does not.

So begin by trusting in divine timing.

You have nothing to lose.

## 54

*Would you wish to take it to your next life?
If not, it would be wise to consider one's actions.
If it is something you would take – you are
wishing and willing to follow you – then
this is the work of the Soul.*

RK


As a channeller, I receive a lot of guidance. Too much to consciously remember ... most of it flows through me. But some messages land deep, slotting into the fabric of my psyche, instant gateways to the Realms – a portal opened.

We don't give this portal away – it is ours to tend and travel through.

## 55

*Life begins, and ends, between
the −1 and the +1. It is a quantum field of
activity ... beyond your wildest imagination.*

MR P.

The space of neutrality lies between the minus-ones and the plus-ones – the gateway to the Realms, and the place of ascension. The access point is within you – through the state of gratitude, where nothing is missing or needed.

It is also the place of healing.

## 56

The soul mourns for where it cannot be now. Not for what it had, or where it was ... but for what it is not being allowed to do *in this moment*.

When we step back in time or project ourselves forward, we pull our soul out of the present moment and become lost between worlds of our own making. Because our soul has a forward-facing job to do. It came here with purpose – to live in *this* time, here and now. This doesn't mean to say we can't heal the past – or the unlived memories of our future. It's just that we do it from the present moment – across all dimensions. Indeed, it is the only way *to* heal.

## 57

*Wisdom is not linear.*

DG

Sometimes we choose to dip into other worlds. To access, or free, the wisdom. Which may be linked to our past or a trauma within, or our lineage or ancestry of origin.

We know when it's ready to be released. Because the forces tell us so. By retrieving it and loving it again. Placing it before us, gently and with utmost care.

And sometimes we explore in other ways, because with the Realms, we can dip into any world of our own making.

But not the worlds of others.

58

Beneath every trauma lies wisdom; concealed by the wound protecting it. Caring for it. Because if we are not ready to collect the gifts of wisdom, the wound will remain in place. Even if we have tended to the rest. Or done all we can.

So we ask the Realms to assist us, and heal the unseen dimensions.

To help us receive what is ready to emerge again.

## 59

*Adjust your reality, before action.*

MR P.

When there is a choice to be made, use your highest grounded frequency and energetic vibration as your base state. The 80/20 rule is a magical combination of reality and Realms – and perfect for ensuring alignment. Eighty percent of your highest vibration – always. Refrain from making important decisions when you find yourself in a lower vibrational state; are experiencing loss of power and spirit; or when your awareness is located primarily in your head or within others. Instead, ease yourself into alignment by inviting your centre of gravity back into your heart, so you can connect with your true energetic reality. Let go and soften the edges – until you can feel the grace of the Realms within you.

Now you are ready for the energetic choice to happen.

## 60

*Respect for other energies
creates a field of protection.*

DG

Just as we ask a tree for permission to approach it, so, too, must we ask for other worlds and realities. *Is this mine to approach? And can I remain centred while doing so?* If the answer is not 100% yes, we step back – remaining in full awareness, thanking the forces of guidance.

We must choose our Realms carefully. What was suitable yesterday may not be so today. A sentence uttered to one person may not be appropriate for another. A proposition, which on the surface appears aligned, might not be so, energetically. Be watchful of the realities you may find yourself inadvertently entering and observe for cul-de-sacs. They can be deceptively enticing.

## 61

I have entered many cul-de-sacs since my awakening. Some I knowingly entered – for learning or healing. Others, my human spirit took me into – to test the status quo, or because I wasn't ready to listen to, or follow, my guidance. And some were concealed: thresholds I *could* have crossed but didn't; my non-action becoming a cul-de-sac of sorts. But irrespective of the reason, a wisdom always emerges for the part of me needing the experience. A necessary detour, to cultivate increased alignment. For when it comes to our path, we can rejoin at any time. To exactly where we're supposed to be.

Indeed, part of us knows we never left the path at all.

# 62

> All is connected and all is One, <u>and</u> one must
> have 'a path'. Without it, one lies in the shadow
> of the undergrowth, never quite seen.
>
> MR P.

You are a human being with a beautiful task: to awaken your soul to this experience of life on Earth – a precious window of opportunity, which can expand and contract somewhat, but is finite. That you walk the planet during this time is no coincidence. Your soul chose it; for this lifetime, and to prepare for the next.

Your path is how the pieces slide together; how the Realms interact.

# 63

*One must give oneself permission to go on the
journey of one's Soul. This permission comes –
and is granted – when the vision is steady.*

AG

We must be willing to seek our path, and to hold it lightly. With eyes open and no expectation or need. Grounded within our imperfection and not-knowing ... inviting these qualities toward us. This is when our vision is steady; when the awareness is ripe.

Because when we go on the mystical journey, we are also preparing for divine disruption and possibilities of connection. Not that we consider this *as* disruption – more so, the act of living, which must not be dismissed. We might like to *think* we need all the answers, but we would be foolish to believe so.

## 64

*There is a journey into oneself. And there is a journey into the new world. The Beauty is revealed in the golden space between.*

**THE ELDERS**

The path responds to your belief in it: a discovery, appearing in each step – signposts leading you forward – the Realms beckoning while delivering back *to* you. As you walk into expansion, your energy lifts, and what was once insurmountable becomes a beautiful piece of a larger puzzle.

You are seeing from within the Realms.

## 65

*What are you willing to leave undone?*

DG

I could never have envisioned the path I now walk, though each step has naturally followed a seamless thread. I have taken my time, to ground. To integrate and heal the multidimensional layers of myself. To discover *my pace*, as I walk between worlds with my writing and work.

At times it has been unsettling. My ego has not liked all of it. But it *does* like the alignment. When in the golden space, there is nowhere I would rather be.

## 66

As we shift through the layers of ourself, emotions can rise. Let them be. They are not 'you' – they are a part of you. Allow them to walk beside you, close – so you can love them.

When we walk the centre of our path, we set our emotions free. Free from the responsibility we gave them. We can't push them away – they will just become louder. Instead, we shepherd them until they, and you, are ready to hear the wisdom.

And then they will go.

## 67

> *The horse has bolted and run*
> *further than the scare of heart.*
>
> RK

We can only walk our path a day at a time. Sometimes, a step at a time. In rhythm and communion with our heart – steady, in tempo with our central beat and magnetic presence. Keep to your heart's pace as you cut through the outside world. The outside world will thank you for it.

## 68

*Master the art of disappearance.*

DG

Your path requires your presence in the world. The question is, which world are you walking in? And, perhaps more importantly, which world are you creating?

Sometimes, we have to disappear from known worlds, in order to create a new one. Not forever, but long enough to explore the wildness of your reality. Create the forces you need to develop these invisible worlds – because, whilst you can hide your creativity from others, you cannot hide it from yourself.

## 69

When you recognise an urgency in yourself, let this grow quietly and consistently into the form of its revelation. Collect all of yourself and see only as far as is needed. Slow it down, and leave the rest to someone else. Take care of what is close and calling your name.

These are the Realms at work.

## 70

*You are more than your
physical body, so much more.*

DG

The world is made of many layers. You are, too. Layers of subtle energies – of frequencies and resonances, vibrating as your life force: the expression of your spirited self.

You can touch your physical body, tune in to your emotional states, connect with your mental awareness – yet it is within your energy fields where the most information is held.

# 71

*The Realms are quantum
fields of information.*

**THE ELDERS**

When the Realms awaken, so do our powers of perception. So the data can be transferred to us – in the background of our awareness and when sleeping. Conglomerations of sensory data and frequency, accumulating – held in spell-like suspension, rippling beyond the fringes of our conscious mind. Knowledge and information – gathering itself – ready for the moment. To be sparked into form.

## 72

*Too much Light blinds the senses,
as much as too little dulls them.*

**THE ELDERS**

The Realms, while magical and elusive, show themselves in consistent ways. A recognition, somewhere within us, of *something* we know to be true. Like a favourite colour we come back to, a Realm calls your name. Not to the exclusion of other Realms, but because your soul knows it. For now, it feels like home.

Your ego-mind may dismiss it and prefer the idea of a different Realm. A shinier, brighter one – with others, perhaps. Let this be okay and for your mind to work this out in its own way.

It is also learning to co-create with the Divine.

## 73

*The Realms, in their formation, await the observing nature of reality.*

**THE ELDERS**

The Realms are not 'outside' us but are triggered within by the external – while also existing everywhere all at once. It is why we can stretch to feel the Realms of beauty, love, divine companionship, freedom – and fall into the Realms of fear and lack.

And the Realms are also what you understand them to be – unique to your combination of ancestry, awareness and grace. To your soul's connection with them. Because to witness the Realms, through the essence of our soul, allows everything to awaken within us.

## 74

*The transcendence to creativity is Divine Grace.*

MR P.

When we connect with a Realm, we discover it in everything – and reality shifts on its axis. After my awakening, I felt the Realms everywhere and wanted to be part of them all. Joy, peacefulness – and importantly, the Realm of healing – were calling my name. The Realms of balance and neutrality gave me safety. Love flooded in; and the Realm of fear – after abating – would intermittently wash through me. And so many more. But what really drew my attention was the subtle change in my writing ... to somewhere beyond myself. Beyond what was happening to, and around, me.

Without knowing it, I was stepping into the Realm of Divine Grace.

## 75

*A simplicity allows access to the Realms,
but it is in <u>creating</u> one actively engages.*

MR P.

The Realms are not complicated – and they make no demands. Rather, they have a playfulness inherent within their simplicity. Every atom and vibration, alive and alert, purposeful and at ease; flowing within itself and the larger rhythms of the Cosmos. Ready for you to engage.

And from this sea of Randomness, you get to choose.

You can create anything you want, for the sheer pleasure of creating.

Because the world holds your gift – in the non-physical *and* the physical.

## 76

*To dismiss any part of oneself, of one's craft, is to admonish the gift itself.*

RK

Our gift – the hidden gem for some and the day's work for others – is to voice truth. The evolving truth wishing to come through us. In this moment. Not instead of the practicalities and what we must tend to, but alongside them. Within them. So your soul can breathe through your heart, and your feet step forward. So your hands can open and your mind let go … to do what it came here to do: to notice and receive inspiration. Your mind is here to help you create.

All you have to do is give permission.

# 77

*Speak your truth – and no less or more.*
*This will always be sufficient.*

**MR P.**

There is a grace to the higher dimensions which allows for nothing but truth. No lies or cross-entanglement of energy. No ego to prove. Simply unfolding moments, inspiring truths from within us. These truths may initially feel awkward: unsettling, provocative, in contrast to the truths of others. Look closer, and you will see they are seamless – and powerful – acts of love.

To catch an energetic lie – a subtle betrayal to ourself or another – and turn it into a slither of truth, is the everyday act of awakening. It is also the work of alchemy.

## 78

*If you do not respect and honour the ability
you have been given – the ability of heart, not
ego-mind – you will lose your power.*

MR P.

Your gift may not look how you thought it would – or require so much from you. It is probably what you have been doing all along, without realising. A quality of your being, held somewhere between your shadow and your light; sitting, as you do, within the Realms of the physical and the non-physical. That you may not be able to name it, is its beauty.

Because some things are sacred.

Some things transcend the ordinary.

79

*You are walking in the unseen worlds.*

DG

When the Realms reveal themselves – as a rainbow or sunset might – we can be tempted to only create the experience within. What the Realms ask, though, is for connection *with them*. In their beauty and also with what is triggered within. *As* the presence of the moment. We may be tempted to see what we *wish* to see – but the Realms enjoy the reciprocal connection of pure vision.

In our pure vision, they respond – to create a moment in consciousness. One which could easily be overlooked, if it wasn't so enticing.

# 80

*It is not a requirement to keep the mind open
to the dimensions, but to enable the mind to enjoy
them. This is the way into the opening Realms.
A mind has a static force. It is called control.
So we turn control into wisdom.*

**THE ELDERS**

We can help our minds by taking care of ourself. We do not want known or lost parts of ourself wandering 'out' of control. So we *invite* our self 'together'. Not tightly, but gently and with loving power – for this can be underestimated work.

We do this so the mind can quieten – and the stillness rise.

Often in such moments we see – quite clearly and suddenly – Realms within us we had not previously been aware of. Only as we gather ourself in this way, do the Realms open for viewing. For the Realms are not viewed with the intellect of the mind, but through the wisdom of the heart.

## 81

When exploring other dimensions, always treat *the wisdom* as the intention – it keeps us safe and grounded: in *our* world, without the risk of 'falling' into another. Benchmark the wisdom, to keep you steady. It creates an important connection and ensures continuity. Storytelling, song writing, the development of journals, prayers and blessings ... these are anchors and openings for the wisdom of the Realms.

## 82

When communing with the metaphysical, it must always be entered through *this* world – though a portal in this dimension, not another. Resist any temptation to expand unnecessarily and incongruently: beyond your body of trust. Recognise the time and place – and your awareness – when 'entering the Realms'. Especially when part of a group. Honouring our alignment and presence ensures our grounded instinct.

It is how we bring the wisdom back.

## 83

*When invisible worlds fall away,
we discover who we have become.*

DG

If I observe my path since my moment of awakening, I see my heart open. I see everything open and ripple out. Like an envelope unfolding. And I also see myself returning – circling from my peripheries, back toward myself. Towards Love. Healing, sorting, reorganising and learning. Clearing the path ahead of me and behind me. Above and below me. So my spirit can breathe.

And sometimes I contract again. I slip out of alignment. Less frequently than before, and when I do, it feels worse. Because I can no longer just exist – the Realms won't let me.

They always nudge me back, into the web of Love.

## 84

*The awakening occurs at the point of
surrender in its extremity, which may be well
after the initial blossoming ... the subtle point
when the changes are accepted.*

AG

We may awaken once, or multiple times in our life. Multiple transitions of awareness and soul integrations – which, ultimately, is what awakening is. My awakening happened instantaneously, and, over weeks and at intervals, over a period of 24 months. As I moved from energetic fight or flight into Love. It was a process of unplugging from perceived reality – into deeper truths of my being. Of shifting through the entanglements and illusions – to find the true, and agile, middle ground. The comfort within my bones.

And it didn't end there. In some ways, it was just the beginning. Because now I had discovered my gift, I had to work out how to share it. How to not sabotage my truth while also being comfortable with the power and possibility of it. Of integrating it into all parts of myself and my life. So I could not only accept it, but embody it. And this has taken time and a lot of patience.

It is actually a process which never ends.

Because there is always more to discover.

85

*The answer lies in the seat of your Soul.*

AG

You will know when you have awakened, because your soul will tell you so. Your soul may also tell you that you have company. Because, even though we have awakened, in our unwillingness to sacrifice our old previous selves, they too come along for the journey.

We are living parallel lives. Which makes for a tiresome time.

Connection with the Realms can provoke fear of separation: we have seen what others – and our previous selves – haven't, and at some point along the path we are called to choose. To surrender to our heart and truth, in our own guided way, or to continue in the growing discomfort. It is a step you, and only you, can take. Alone – *and* connected. With your heart in your hands, beating.

And when you *do* transcend, you make a discovery. That you lost nothing of yourself and gained it all. That your old selves are always there; in the Realms, with you. In handing yourself wholeheartedly to your soul, you release all previous – and precious – versions of yourself. You release them to the Light – so you can *be* the wisdom within them.

## 86

*You can begin anew. In all circumstances,
you can begin anew.*

AG

There are many ways to enter the Realms – innumerable entry points. *And* we are given the opportunity to consider our life anew. This, too, is a Realm, if we choose it. A doorway into increased wellbeing and an unhindered life.

Into a well-positioned body and oriented soul.

Our frustration and struggle indicate when we are out of alignment. A resistant body and a restless mind are signs of a misplaced soul – and the need for a moment of surrender.

It is the moment to begin anew ...

... and return to yourself again.

# 87

*The world you carry is the one on your back.*
*But the world you offer is the one in your heart. So*
*a choice must be made: open your heart, or carry*
*your load. One can be placed down before you.*
*One, you can never remove. Which will it be?*

MR P.

We live in a material world, but it's the invisible loads which weigh heaviest.

A requisite for entering the Realms is to release the loads which brought you to the threshold. We cannot take forward what was meant for past timelines. Because the Realms operate on frequency and Love – and Love invites no baggage, no 'shoulds', no quantifying of existence or being.

So we let it all be. As it is. We breathe ... and we expand. And with our hand to our heart, we ask *it* what to pick up. Just one thing; and we go from there.

What you need will always be provided for – but the mind will never believe it. We have to *become* the path to know this as true.

## 88

*The Soul's orientation is toward the Light.*

AG

When the wisdom lands, an illumination occurs. We experience a frequency shift. Usually after or at the point of letting go. Because we are in our heart energy; and when our body is in harmony, taking its presence from the Light of our soul, an alignment happens. Consciously or unconsciously, everything reorients.

This, like the Realms, can happen in myriad of ways.

## 89

*A disbelief in life is what keeps people trapped.*

MR P.

There have been moments since my awakening when I have felt like I've been punched in the chest. Winded, floored, knocked breathless across many dimensions. By big events and smaller circumstances – in the physical world, and non-physically, within visions and healing.

It is the wind blowing me in to place. Into soul alignment.

It is *meant* to knock us breathless – so we catch the full force of our soul.

And are held by it.

Connected, at a higher frequency.

As reality shifts around us.

## 90

When we move into a more metaphysical experience, the unexpected happens: we become more *physical*. More awake to the felt world around us. Increasingly grateful for it and connected to it. At a cellular level. We crave deeper levels of touch, to *feel* the rain on our face and back ... and this extraordinary planet beneath our feet. We appreciate the presence of both pleasure *and* pain, aware they are fleeting *and* proof of our existence. Aware, too, that we won't always be able to gaze upon our loved ones, or feel them in this way.

In going beyond, we land firmly where we're meant to be.

## 91

> *What you have not done is follow your wisdom. You have followed your fears, and so you got stuck.*
>
> MR P.

You don't need all the answers. These will come in their own time – with hindsight, and with a softening within. For fear exists in the mind of the unknown, and not in the heart of the known. You also don't need the fears of others, though these may come with good intention. Others also carry wounds and may feel separated from Source. From their hearts and gifts. From their path. So we release the fears to the Light. As often as is necessary.

Cleanly, softly and with care for all involved.

Returning to ourself. As a gracious act of Love.

## 92

*Love takes forth what it is given.*

AG

With the Realms, we don't look for 'proof'. To do so causes energy leakage – and distance from ourself. Fear is love disconnected from itself. So when this happens, we allow it to be. To find its way back to our heart. Because two things can be true at the same time.

Instead, we turn to our friends, creativity, laughter and movement. True love teaches us how to be in its presence – and humour, loving kindness and loyalty are bridges: godly qualities if truly understood.

## 93

*The magic creates the momentum.*

DG

When the Realms awaken, so too does our connection to the flow state. Our cells oscillate at a different frequency and energies connect in a more effortless way. We experience a roaming flow, as things fall into place, and time mysteriously appears and disappears. Our gaze becomes soft and receiving – rather than a 'looking' one. Our actions are considered and effortless, as our energy radiates through our heart. An energy of unhindered awareness and love.

We are in the sacred allowing of creativity and wellness.

It is our natural state of being.

### 94

The flow state can be our everyday disposition – in the background of our awareness, limitless and present. Not suppressed or permitted only 'when things are going well'.

Most of my truly magical and extraordinary events have occurred during times of 'crisis'. This is, for me, when I have dropped into the deepest flow state – doorway after internal doorway opening, to reveal synchronicities and possibilities I could never have imagined, or wouldn't previously have let in. With my mind quiet and my spirit now flowing through me, 'the crisis' becomes a magical unfolding of emergent wisdom. Everything rises to a higher divine order, despite how it may look to others.

When the mind goes quiet, for whatever reason, Realms can awaken within us.

## 95

> *The Realms are reflections of the stages of evolution of the Soul. And the Soul cannot be separated from Source – just as your spirit or breath cannot be separated from you.*
>
> AG

We can perceive the Realms in untold ways – a subjective reflection of a Source present in all we see. Whether in our mind's eye or with eye-sight. We can think of the Realms as vibrations or levels of consciousness; of lighter or denser energies – and the fullest spectrum in between. Or as matter, held within form. We can give them words, of metaphysical guidance or scientific knowledge – or any language of our choosing. Indeed, one's language or country could be viewed as a Realm – different from, or connected to, the language or country of another. Just as cells divide and harmonise with one another – a 'language' also spoken between them.

The more we see, the more connected we become.

Our work is to become comfortable with this.

And to hold the vibration with flow.

96

*There is a layer, Child, where we merge,
and there are clear differentiations too.*

AG

In the moments of transition, glimpses appear. As the Realms overlap and integrate – and then move apart. When channelling, and in life in general, I overlap my physical and non-physical Realms, and also include many others: the Realms of beauty, adventure and exploration, of insight, energetic alignment, and so many more. All moving and adjusting within me. This is how we, as humans, come to be: by 'stacking Realms' – energetic layers and realities we *choose* to embody ... or which, if not consciously attended to, embody us.

When we begin to identify the energy of a Realm within us, we have the choice: to embody it more fully, or to choose another more beckoning one. One which harmonises our frequency and settles our senses; leaving us inspired, yet with feelings of safety and belonging, of truth. This is also how we transmute energy and transform to higher Realms of consciousness, while becoming increasingly human, to ourselves and towards each other.

# 97

> *The task of the human spirit*
> *is to remain intact.*
>
> **THE ELDERS**

The Realms are already awake within you. Divine layers of Light, coded information and Love – woven into unseen energies within you. Your beautiful human form: an invitation to discover what it means to live without fear; for your spirit to radiate and your Love to shine. Tread gently as you navigate these steps to your heart. But go fearlessly to meet yourself in all of your multidimensionality. You won't look back, except with admiration for the path beneath your feet.

## 98

*You know the way and the way knows you.*

MR P.

The journey begins before the first step is taken. It begins within your heart, at your soul's insistence. Something within you is ready to do differently.

As this inner world meets the outer, a realignment occurs. Pay attention to what you take with you: what you pack in the material and invisible worlds. You need far less and also far more than you think.

Gather what's precious, what heals – and what unites.

# 99

*Today is as important as any day. Today has all the power to change a reality for the better or the worse. In energy, all things are equal. Master this for yourself and you contribute to the whole.*

**THE ELDERS**

One, two, four or more people change the vibration of the world.
    One by one, we are awakening.
    One energetic step at a time.

## 100

*Let the Realms come to meet you.*

**THE ELDERS**

Metaphysical information is the poetic in motion; and wanting to heal ourselves and our lives is an act of power and grace. I bow to everyone on this journey – myself included. Seize the moments of divine inspiration – they are alchemical opportunities and blessings, often overlooked. Allow the illuminations. Distinct and informative, vast and simple, magical and practical – allow them to be.

Allow the beauty.
*Allow the illumination.*

The magic happens
when we *hold it lightly.*

Towards the beginning of my spiritual awakening, I visited the College of Psychic Studies in London for a weekly course on *'energetic grounding and protection'*. The college has a small but beautiful library – a powerful vortex of energy. The first week I arrived, while waiting for the course to begin, I was 'moved' to a bookcase, my arm was raised and a book was taken from the shelf: *Journey to Ixtlan: The Lessons of Don Juan* by Carlos Castaneda. I glanced at it and put it back. The second week, I had exactly the same experience, and this time I sat down to read a page or two. The third week, I got the message and took it out on loan. A Realm opened for me.

To date, I have taken three core teachings from this book: the influence and power of unseen energy; the reference to '*we hardly ever realise that we can cut anything out of our lives, anytime, in the blink of an eye*' (and the corresponding ability to introduce anything *into* our lives in such a way); and the invitation to release '*all personal history*'.

It is this third teaching which comes to me now, in writing these final words: a release that so many of us find hard to do. Because our personal history contains so much love – lived and unlived. Seen and unseen. Physical *and* divine. But if we can be courageous enough to let it all go, we allow it to become. Transmuted and transformed. Into pure essence; into our life now. As a breathing, moving force of Love.

When we see the beauty in each step, it becomes a dance with the Divine.

My wish is that this book, in some way, may open a Realm for you.

# With Gratitude

This book would not have been possible without the assistance and wisdom of my spiritual guides. The quotes in this book are from the many pages of personal guidance I have received and metaphysical information I have collected – each guide, or collection of guides, offering their unique perspective, intelligence and care. Together, they invite a collective energy and message for us all. My gratitude for their presence and love extends beyond words.

**AG** – *Archangel Guidance*
**THE ELDERS** – *A group of six energetic Beings and Sages*
**MR P.** – *The Spirit of Plato*
**RK** – *The Spirit of Rudyard Kipling*
**DG** – *Divine Guidance*

I am also grateful for the work of Carlos Castaneda. My reference to his words: '*We hardly ever realise that we can cut anything out of our lives, anytime, in the blink of an eye*' can be found in his books *Journey to Ixtlan: The Lessons of Don Juan* and *The Wheel of Time: The Shamans of Ancient Mexico, Their Thoughts About Life, Death and the Universe.*

# Acknowledgements

I am deeply grateful for the support I have received while writing and publishing this book.

To Kate Adams – I will treasure the summer days we spent fine-tuning and exploring the passages in this book. Your combination of lightness of touch and depth of professional insight has been invaluable in shaping this book into what it wished to become.

To Jenny Cattermole – it has been a joy to work with you again. I have loved it. Your attention to detail, enthusiasm and care in copy-editing this work is deeply appreciated.

To Therese Vandling (and a big thank you to Anna Ruiz for the introduction) – I feel this book chose you for its cover. Your beautiful designs have brought it visually to life and I am truly grateful for the creativity and care you have contributed.

And to my friends and family – my heartfelt gratitude, to each and every one of you. Your love and encouragement mean the world to me.

# Related Works

Two of RK's quotations are taken from my previously published work, *A Metaphysical Conversation with Rudyard Kipling: On Writing, the Afterlife and the Spirited Human*. The quotation in passage 54 is from page 60, 'Communing with the muse', and the quotation in passage 76 is from page 166, 'The writer's instinct'.

Further channelled guidance on the subjects of Randomness, the −1/+1 philosophy and the 80/20 rule can be found in my first book, *The Teachings of Mr P*.

## About the Author

Delilah Sullivan is a spiritual writer, energy
channel and teacher based in the UK.

Her work between the physical and non-physical
worlds brings healing, alignment and insight to
many. Inspired by beauty and informed by energy,
she invites us to connect with the wisdom of our
soul and the energy of our spirit, to live a full and
awakened life.

www.delilahsullivan.com

Printed in Dunstable, United Kingdom